Martin Luther King

Written by Verna Wilkins
Illustrated by Lynne Willey

W

This edition 2012

Franklin Watts
338 Euston Road
London NW1 3BH

Franklin Watts Australia
Level 17/207 Kent Street
Sydney NSW 2000

Text first published as *Famous People, Famous Lives:*
Martin Luther King in 1998

ISBN: 978 1 4451 0869 8

A CIP catalogue record for this book
is available from the British Library.

Dewey Decimal Classification: 323.1'196073'092

Series editor: Sarah Peutrill
Original series editor: Sarah Ridley
Artwork: Lynne Willey (line), Lisa Williams (colour)

Consultant: Dr Anne Millard

Printed in China ·

Franklin Watts is a division of Hachette Children's Books, an
Hachette UK company.
www.hachette.co.uk

Chapter 1

On a Saturday morning in 1929, Martin Luther King was born in the south of the United States of America. He had a brother and a sister and his family was quite wealthy.

One day, when he was six, Martin went out to play at his friend's house. His friend's mother looked at him strangely and said to him, "You boys are old enough for school now – you can't play here any more. Go away."

Martin was very upset and ran home.

"Why," he asked his mother, "can't I play with my friend any more?"

His mother held him close and explained. "Some white people are made to think that they are better than black people. You are as good as anyone else, and don't you ever forget that."

Come, my dear.

Martin began to notice signs that read, "No Colored Allowed. Whites only."

He learned from his parents that those signs meant that black children had to go to schools that were shabby. They meant that black people could not eat where white people ate.

He learned also that black people had to sit at the back of the bus.

One day, on a shopping trip, he raced
to a lift. It had beautiful shiny buttons he
could push.

"Let's use this one," he said to his mother.

"Shush," she said to him. "This one is not
for us. We must use that one."

She pointed to an ugly, old lift. This made
Martin unhappy.

Chapter 2

Martin's parents sent him to a good school. He was very clever and finished school three years earlier than was usual.

Then he went to university. He made many good friends there and worked hard. He also loved clothes!

One summer, he took a holiday job in a northern city, a long way from home. Here there were no signs saying, "Whites Only, No Colored." Martin felt happy. He decided then that he wanted black people to to be treated the same as white people, all over America.

He decided to become a minister when he left university. In church, he would preach for a change in the laws.

FRUIT PICKING
WORKERS NEEDED

After he had passed his first degree, Martin went on to study theology. He also thought about ways to change the unfair laws against black people.

In 1951, Martin graduated from college with the highest grades in his year. His parents gave him a brand new car. He was delighted.

Then Martin fell in love with a music student. He married Coretta when he was twenty-four years old.

He still continued his studies. In 1955, he was awarded a special degree, called a Doctorate in Theology, and became Dr. Martin Luther King.

Chapter 3

Now that he had finished his studies, Martin became a minister of a church. As he had planned, he preached and prayed about the unfair laws against black people. He and thousands of others marched against these unequal laws.

Eventually, one law was changed so that black children and white children could go to the same schools. Martin was pleased with this success. But there was more to be done.

Then, not long afterwards, a woman called Rosa Parks was on her way home from work.

She climbed onto a bus and sat down in the black section.

When the bus was full, the driver ordered the black people to stand so that the whites could sit down. Rosa Parks refused and the police arrested her.

Rosa was found guilty and fined, even though she had done nothing wrong. This made many black people angry. Martin saw a chance to organise black people to change this law.

So black people refused to use the buses. Some shared cars to get to work, and some walked everywhere. The white people who owned the buses lost lots of money.

This is good exercise

Eventually, almost a year later, the law was changed and black people could use the buses in the same way as whites could.

Still, Martin continued to preach against unequal laws. By 1957, the whole world had begun to take an interest in his work. He led many marches of black people fighting for better rights in America.

He was arrested over one hundred times for his part in the marches.

Chapter 4

By now, Coretta and Martin had four children and the family moved back to the town where Martin was born. Here Martin preached at his father's church and enjoyed spending time with his family.

He continued to organise protest marches, because there was so much more to be done.

Even though some laws had been changed, black people were still being treated unfairly. This made Martin sad.

So, Martin continued to organise marches. Sometimes he was arrested on these marches. Once he was locked in a dark cell by himself for nine days.

Eventually, even young children joined the protests. A large group of them marched against the laws stopping black people from using some restaurants, libraries and toilets.

The police ordered powerful hoses to be turned on them and many were hurt. Some politicians were horrified at how events were turning out. So, ninety days later, the laws were changed.

Still there was more to be done.

In the summer of 1963, a huge number of people, both black and white, marched peacefully in Washington. It was on this day that Martin Luther King gave his most famous speech.

"I have a dream," he said, "that my four children will one day live in a nation where they will be judged, not by the colour of their skin, but by the content of their character..."

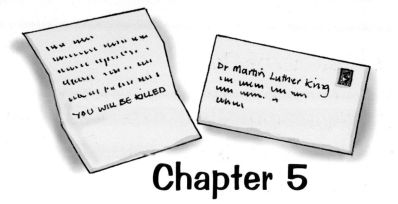

Chapter 5

Around this time, Martin received a series of letters saying, "You will be killed."

"I don't think I'm going to live to forty," he told Coretta, his wife. They were worried. Change was so slow.

However, there was some good news soon after as Martin was awarded the Nobel Peace Prize. He felt encouraged and continued his difficult task.

Daily News

Martin Luther King wins Nobel Peace Prize.

Martin then began his next campaign. Very few black people were registered to vote in elections. "You must register to vote," he begged them. "That way black people will be able to influence the government more."

Martin and his supporters organised even more marches. Many times they were stopped by police. And many times violence erupted.

By this time, more white people were joining the marchers. They realised that America needed to change.

Some white people were attacked for joining the black marchers. Sometimes policemen tried to stop the marchers by force.

As a result of all the work done by Martin Luther King and his followers, the Voting Rights Act was passed in 1965. At last black people had the right to vote. Martin was in Washington D.C. to witness the occasion.

In April 1968, Martin travelled with friends to Memphis, Tennessee. Here, he spoke to two thousand followers. He spoke peacefully. "I have a dream," he said, "... that the brotherhood of man will become a reality..."

After this successful day, Martin was relaxing on the balcony of his motel before dinner. Suddenly someone shot him. His friends rushed him to hospital but doctors could not save his life.

Further Facts
Martin Luther King Day

As Martin was such a powerful leader, who achieved so much good, he is remembered every year with a public holiday in the USA. His life is celebrated on the third Monday in January.

Martin Luther King Foundation

This organisation aims through education to continue Martin's fight for equal rights for all people. As Martin said, "Together we must learn to live as brothers/sisters or together we will be forced to perish as fools."

Who killed Martin Luther King?

James Earl Ray was found guilty of the murder of Martin Luther King. He was sentenced to ninety-nine years in prison. However, he later claimed that he was innocent and blamed another man. It is said that he was visited in prison by relatives of Martin Luther King who believed his story. However, he was never granted another trial and died in prison in 1998.

Some important dates in Martin Luther King's lifetime

1929 Martin Luther King is born in Atlanta, Georgia, USA.

1948 Martin gains his first degree in Sociology.

1951 Martin studies to be a minister.

1953 Coretta Scott and Martin Luther King get married.

1954 Martin becomes minister of a church in Atlanta.

1955 Boston University awards Martin his Doctorate in Theology.

1955 Martin organises marches to highlight the case of Rosa Parks.

1958 Martin finishes his first book, *Stride toward Freedom*.

1960 Martin moves to the Ebenezer Baptist Church where he preaches with his father.

1961–3 Martin fights many campaigns to improve life for black people in the USA.

1963 Before a crowd of 200,000 people, Martin gives his 'I have a dream' speech.

1964 Martin awarded Nobel Peace Prize.

1965 The Voting Rights Act is passed as a result of all the hard work of Martin and his supporters.

1968 Martin is shot dead on April 4th.

Quiz

Can you remember?

1. When was Martin Luther King born?
2. What were some of the things that black people had to do separately to white people?
3. What did Martin want to be when he left university?
4. What did Martin Luther King preach about?
5. What did Rosa Parks do?
6. How many children did Martin have?
7. When was the Voting Rights Act passed and who did it mean had the right to vote?
8. What prize was Martin awarded?
9. When was Martin Luther King shot?
10. What had he been doing before he was shot?

Answers on page 32

Glossary

colored In the USA, this word was used to describe people whose ancestors came from Africa originally.

degree An award given to someone who has completed their studies at university.

fine A sum of money that has to be paid as the punishment for doing something wrong.

minister The name for the person who leads church services and who preaches to the worshippers.

Nobel Peace Prize A prize given every year to the person who has been most successful in making people behave peacefully.

register to vote Sign a piece of paper so that you are allowed to vote.

rights Equal rights aim to give people the same chances in life.

theology The study of religion.

Index

Quiz answers

1. 1929
2. Use different schools, restaurants and lifts and sit separately on buses
3. A minister
4. Unfair laws against black people
5. Refuse to stand up on the bus to make room for white people
6. Four children
7. 1965, black people had the right to vote
8. Nobel Peace Prize
9. 1968
10. Giving a speech